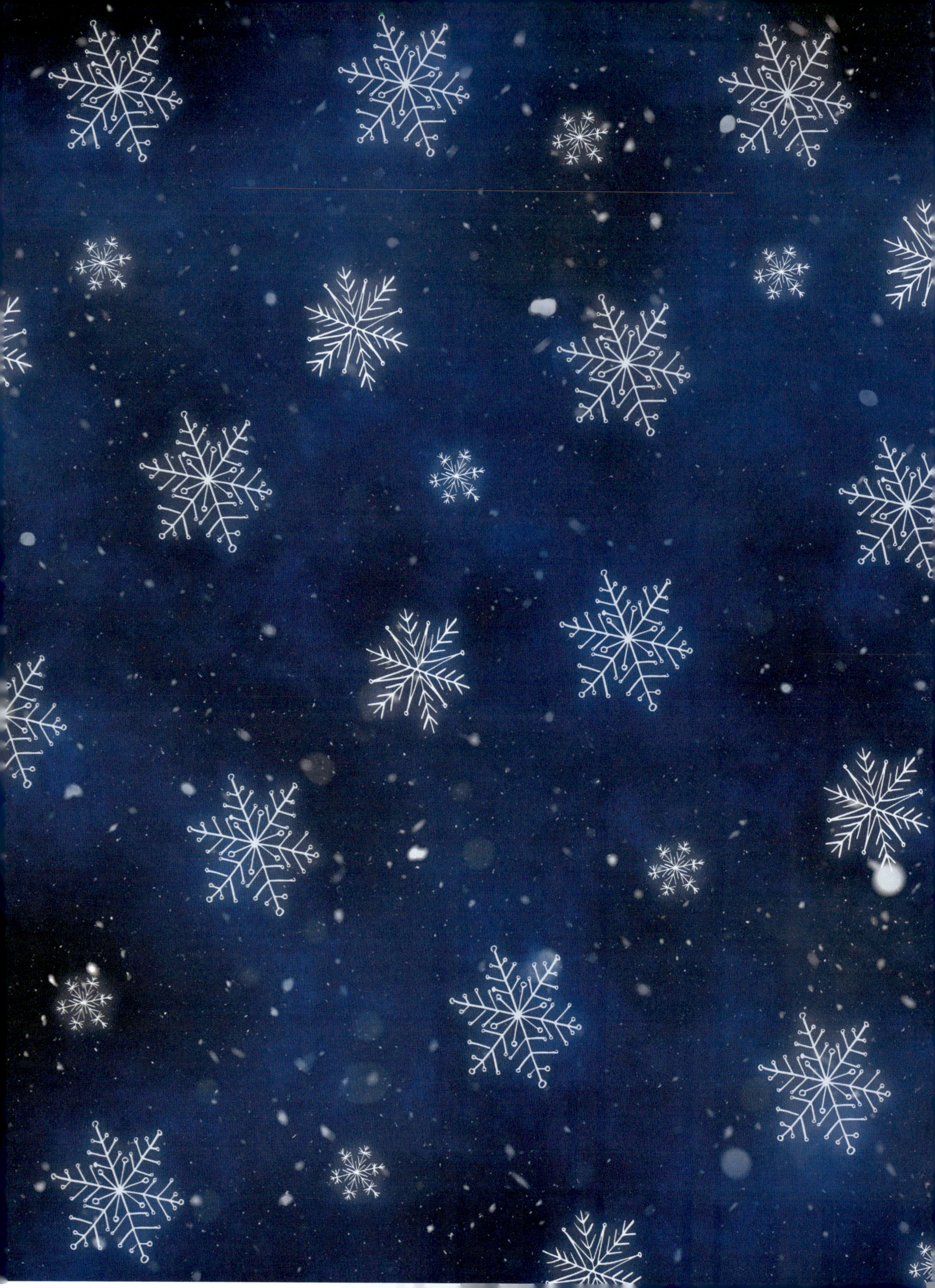

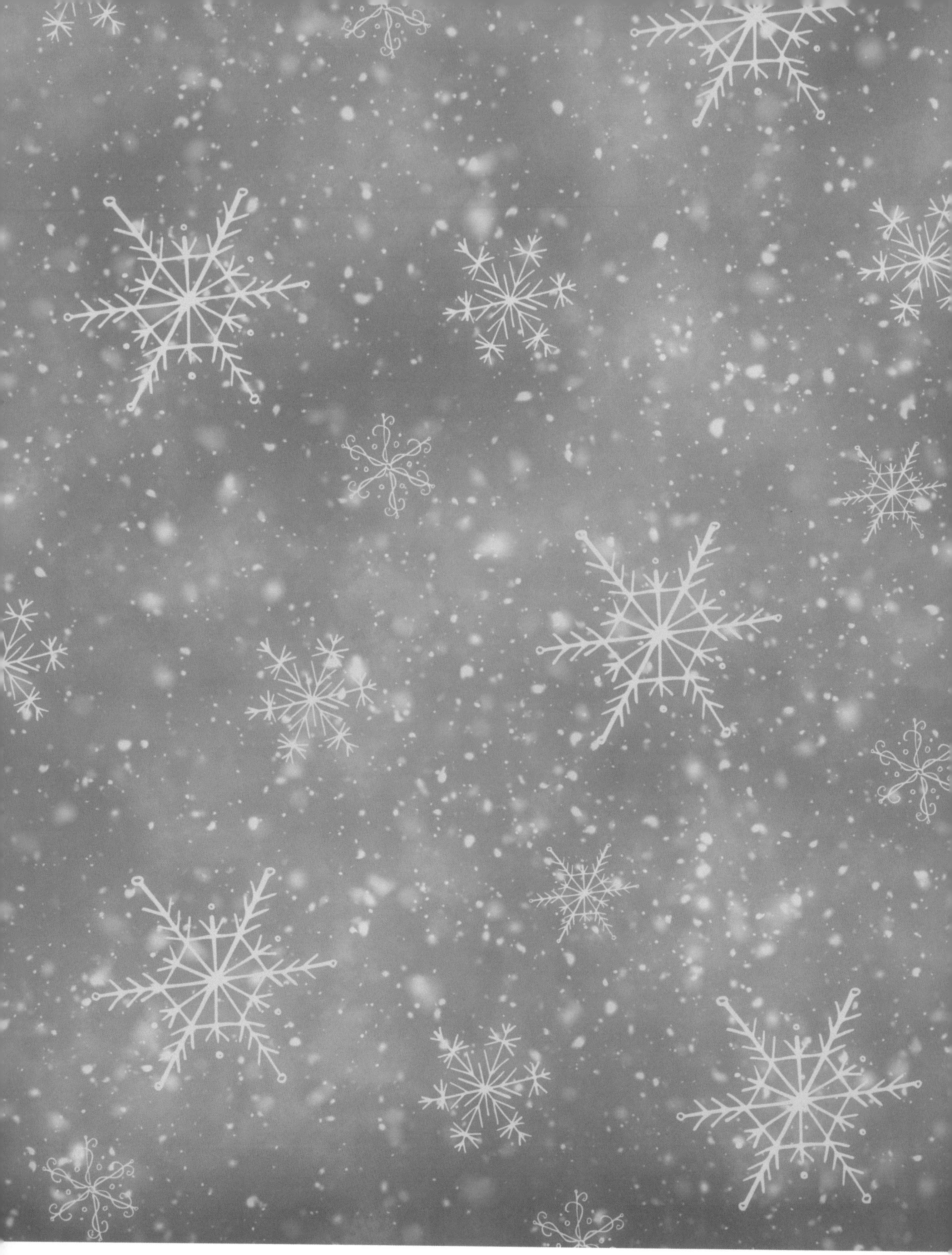

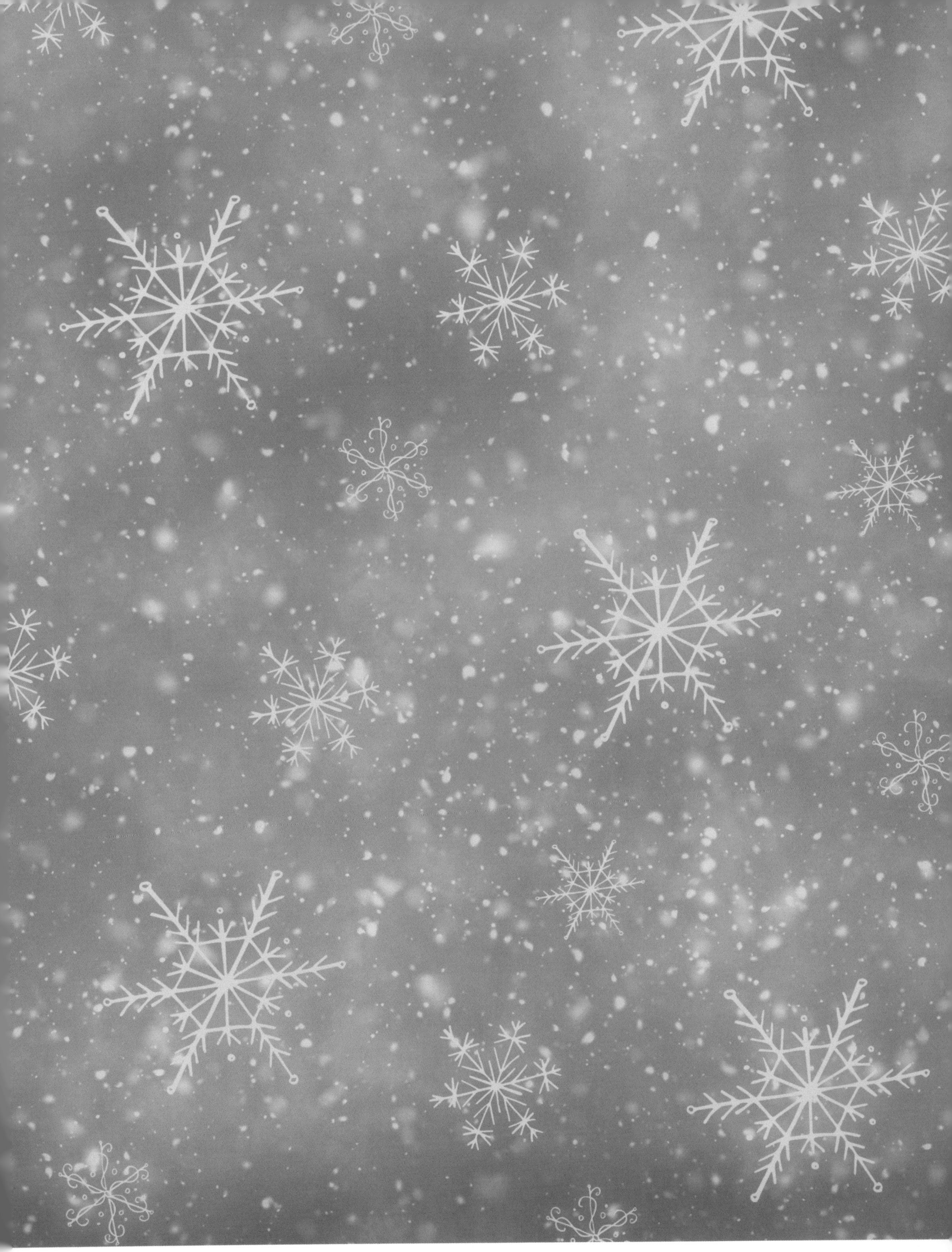

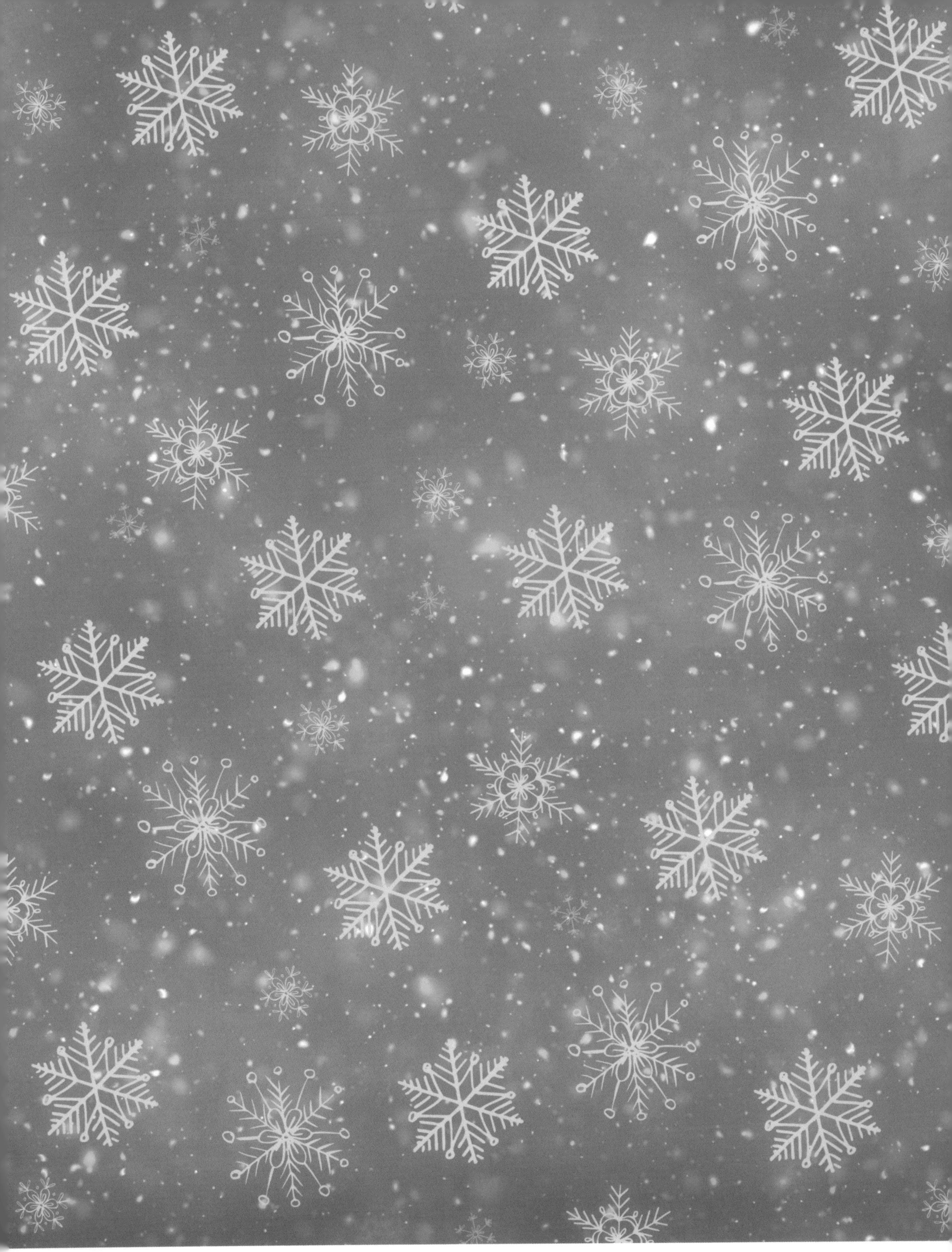

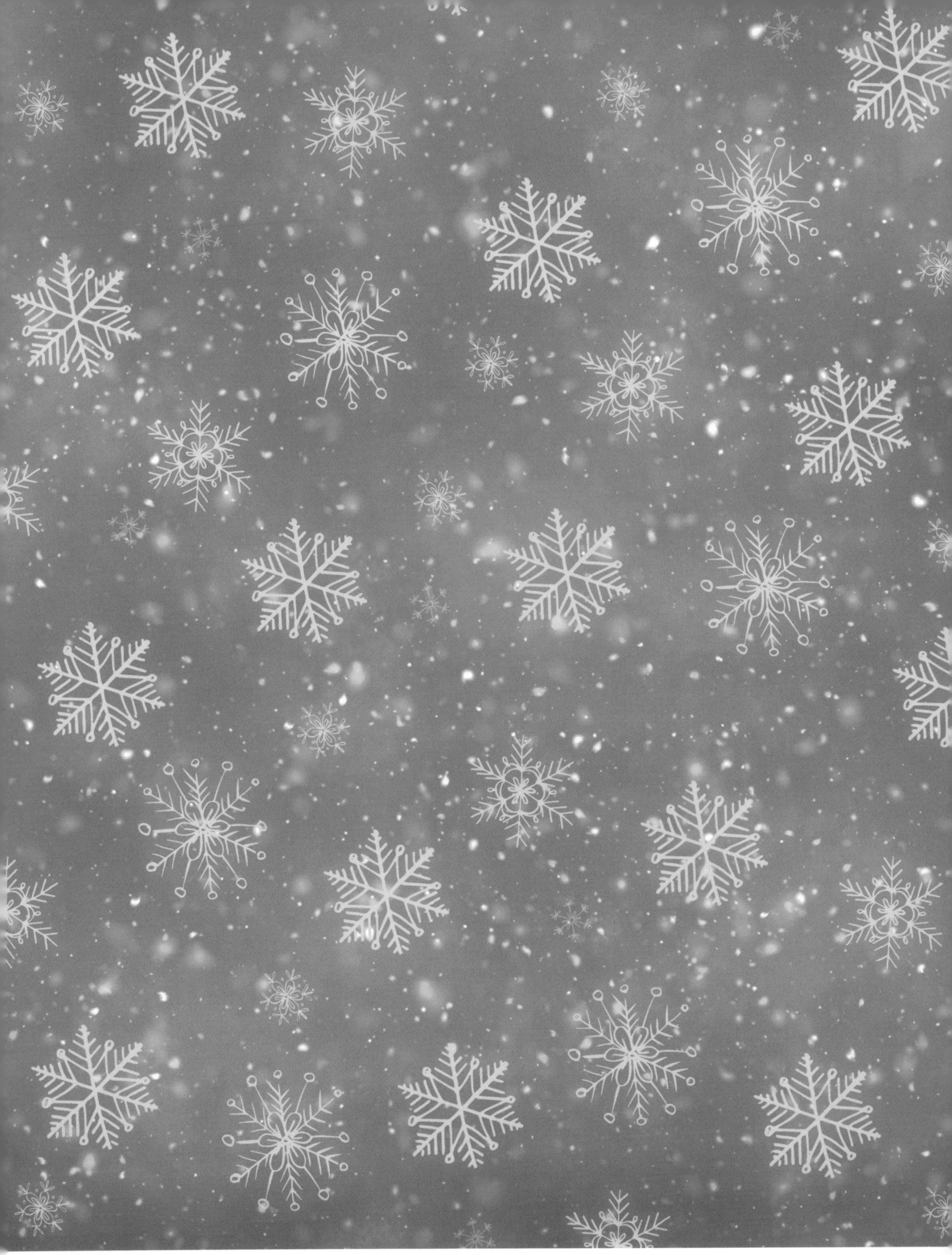

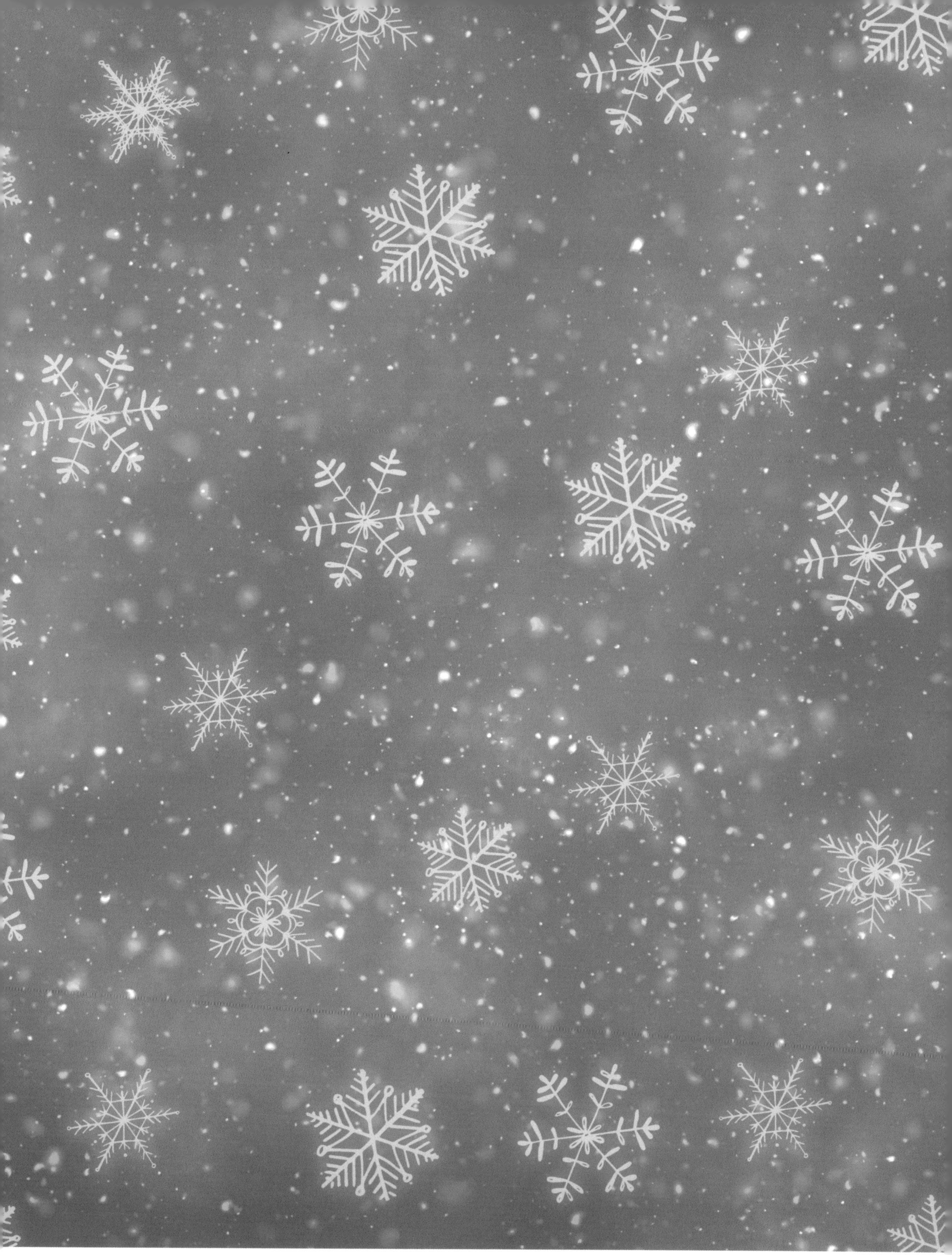

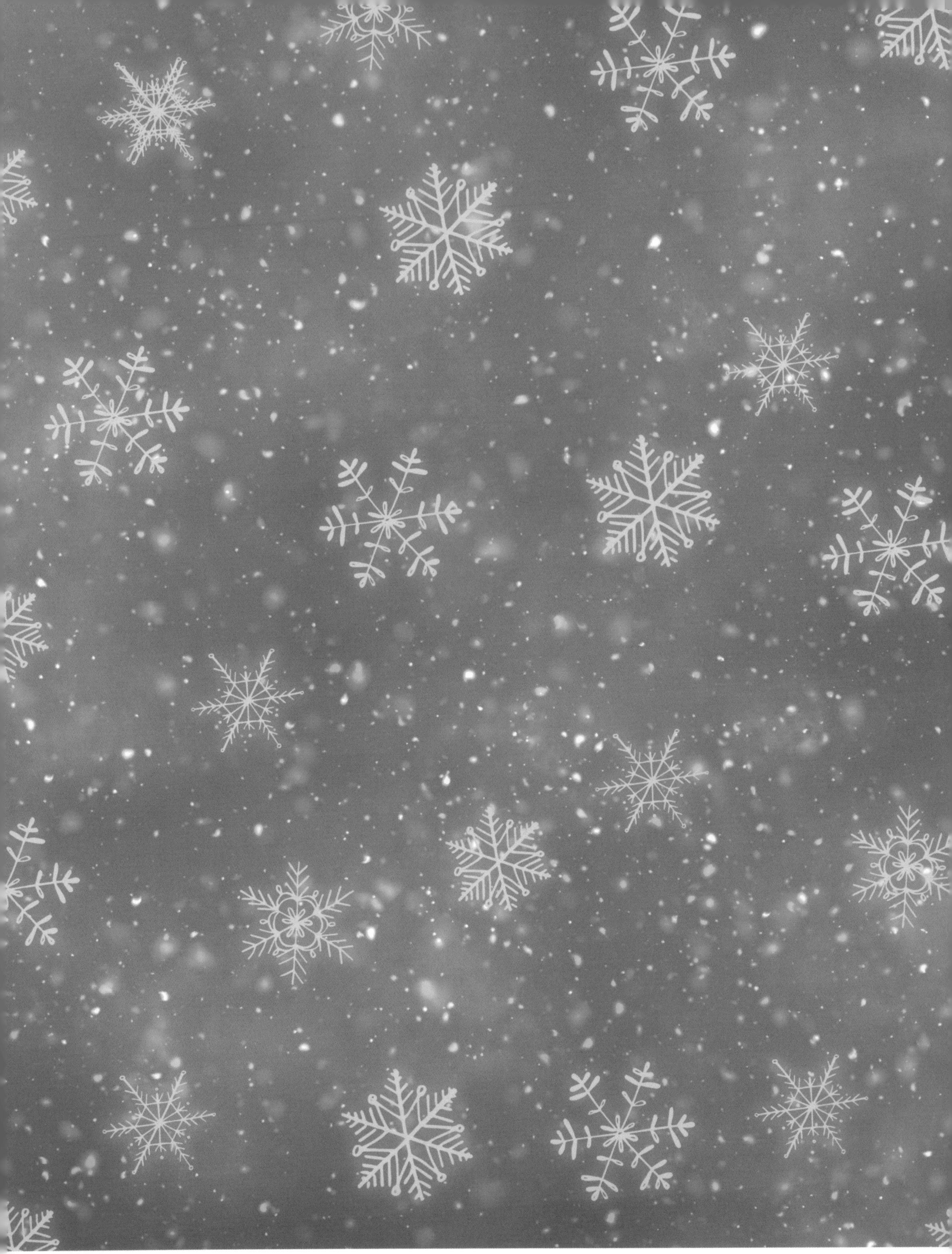

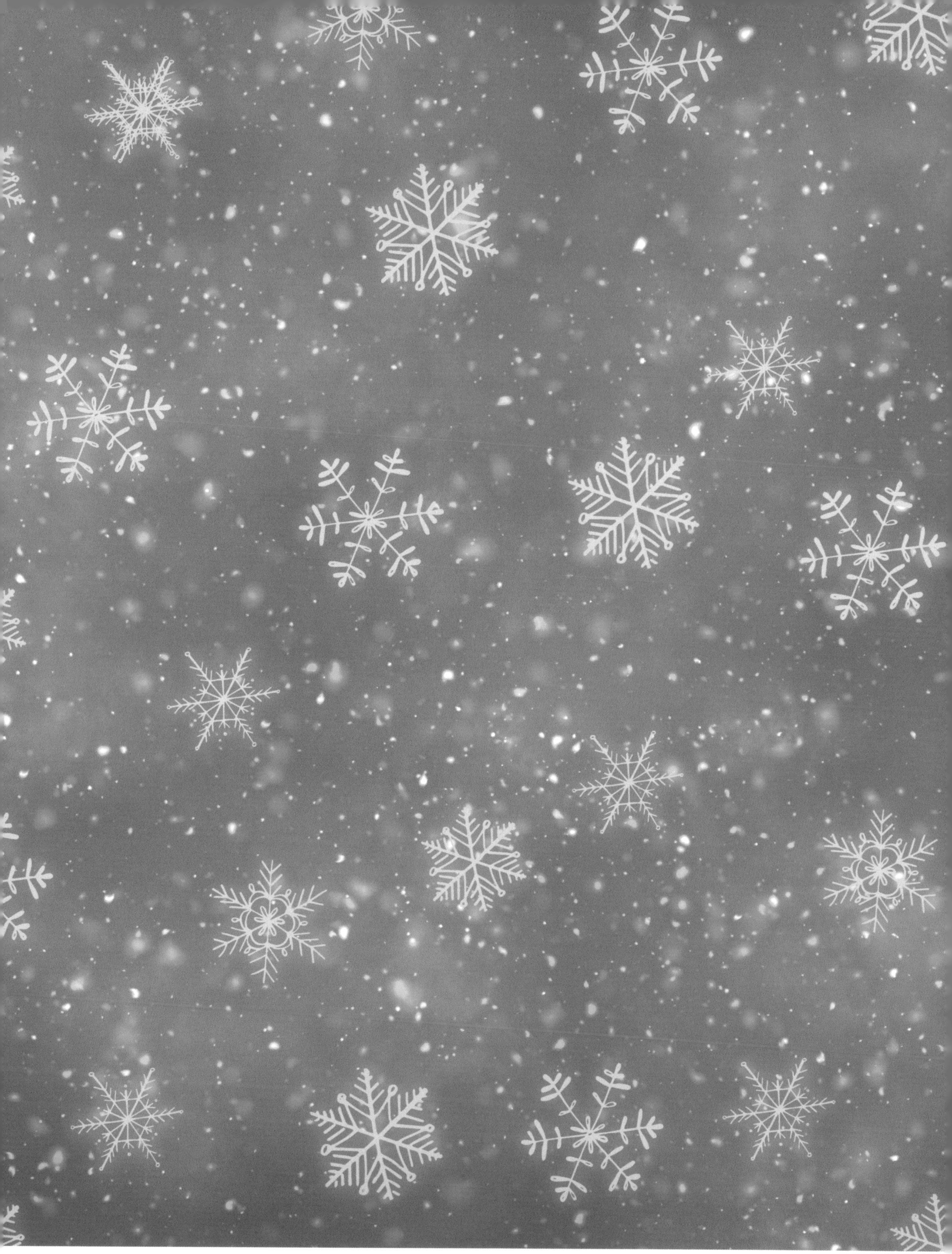

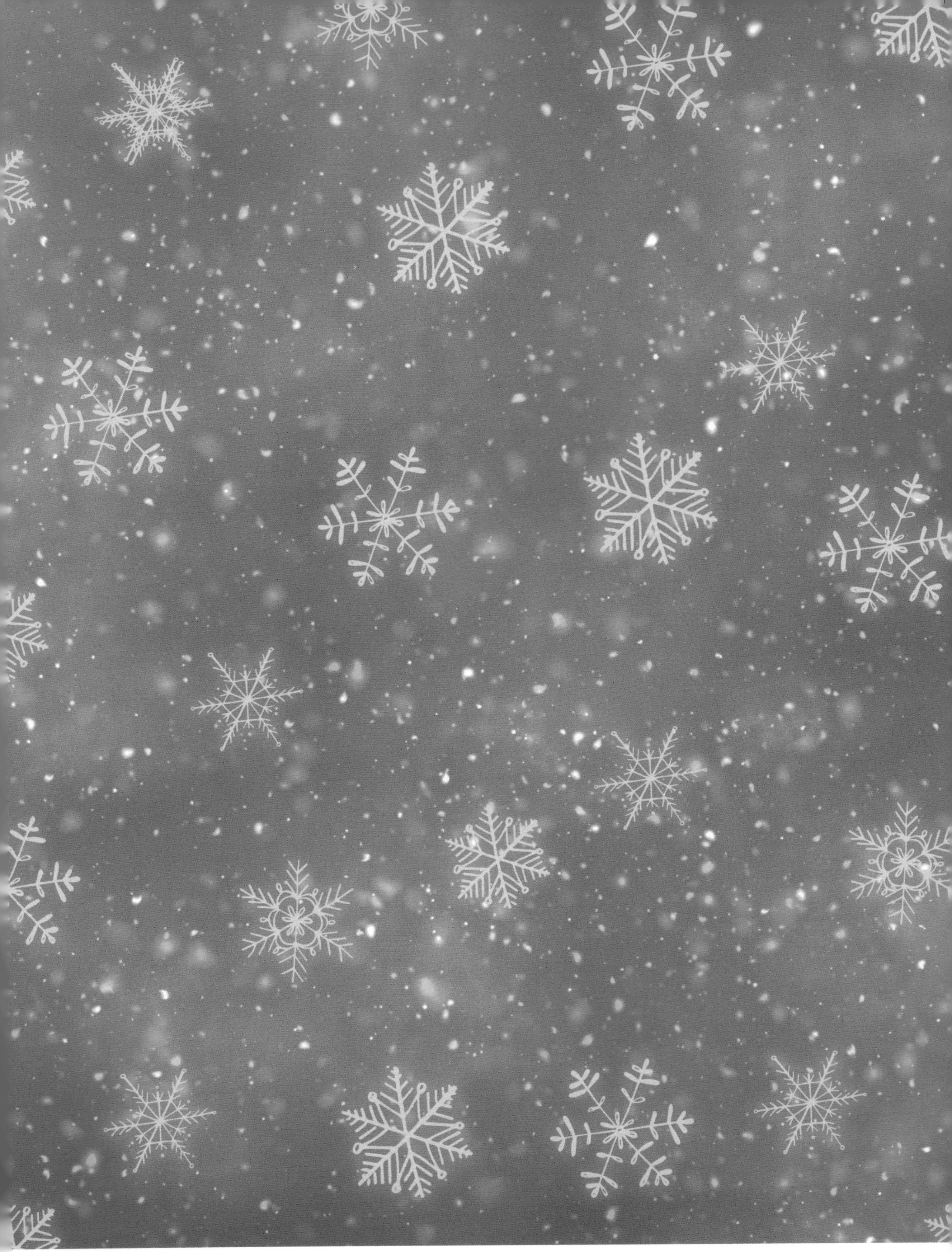

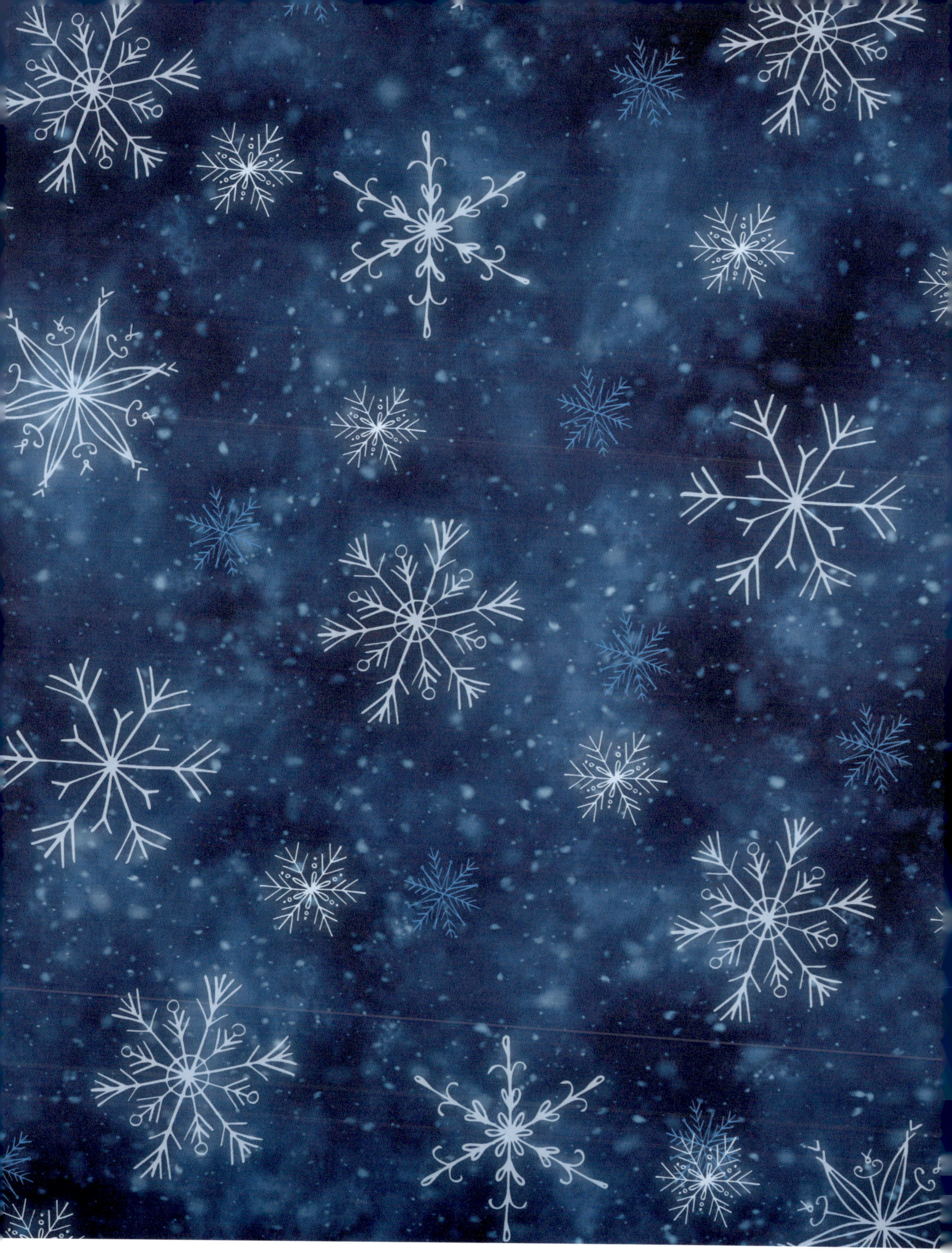

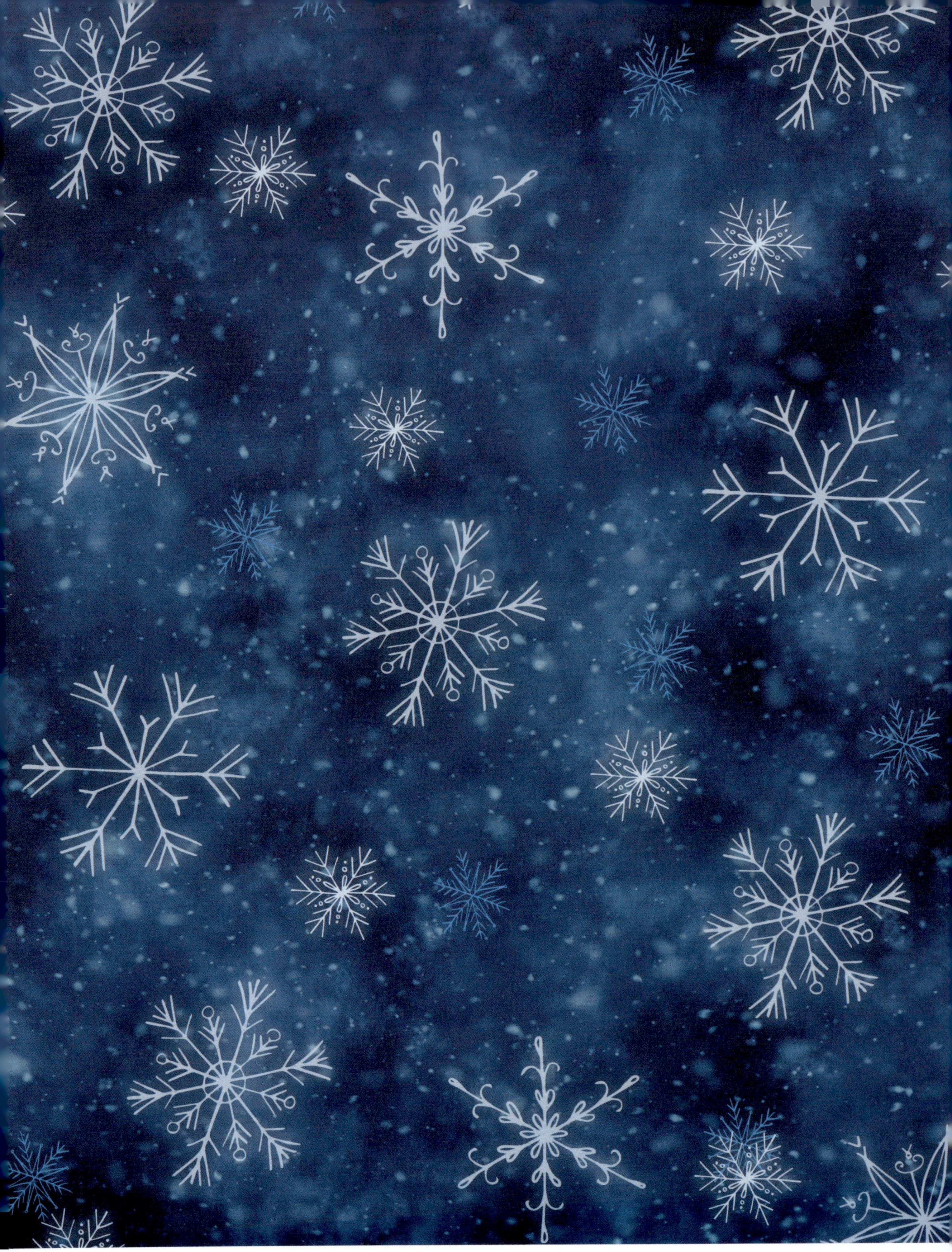

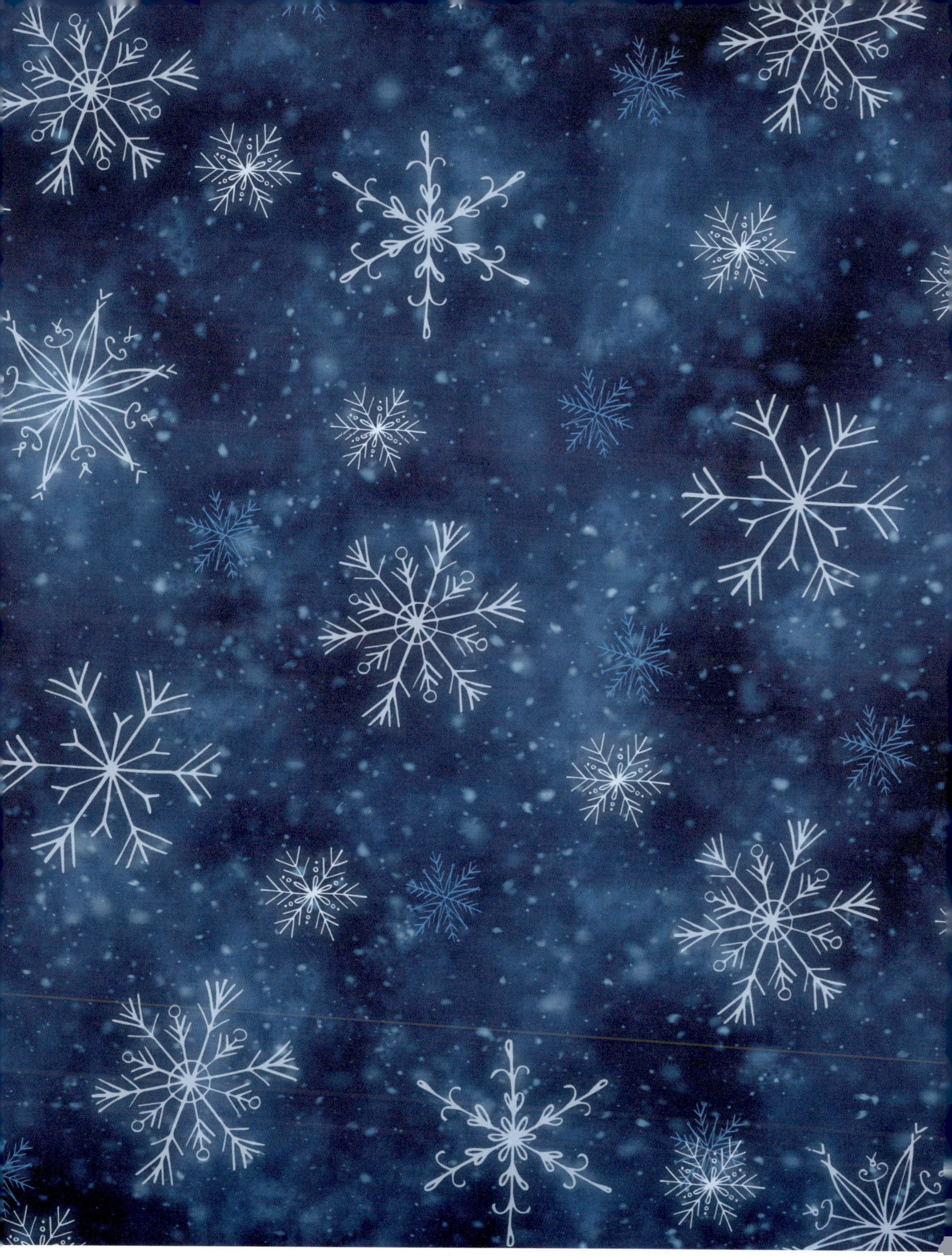

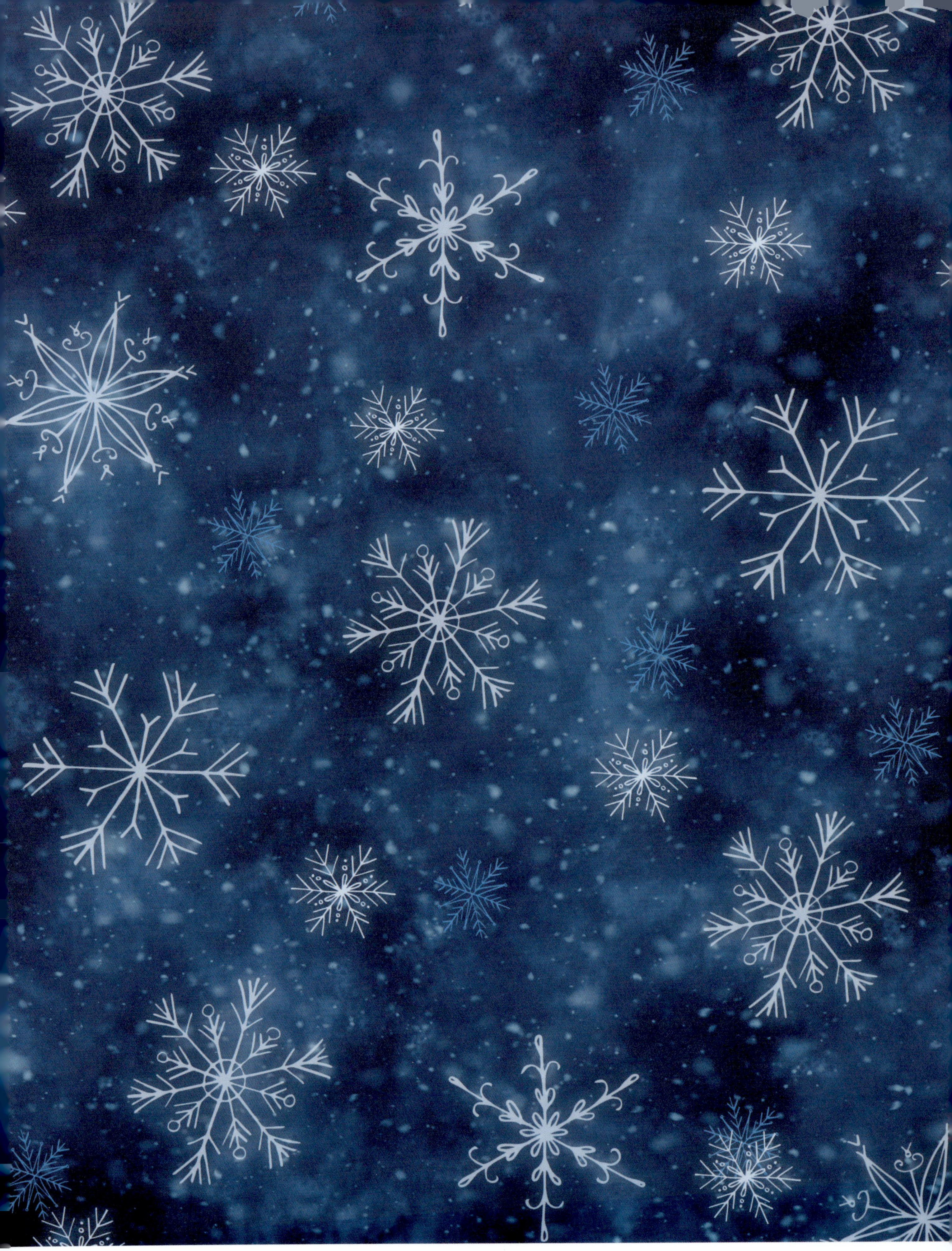

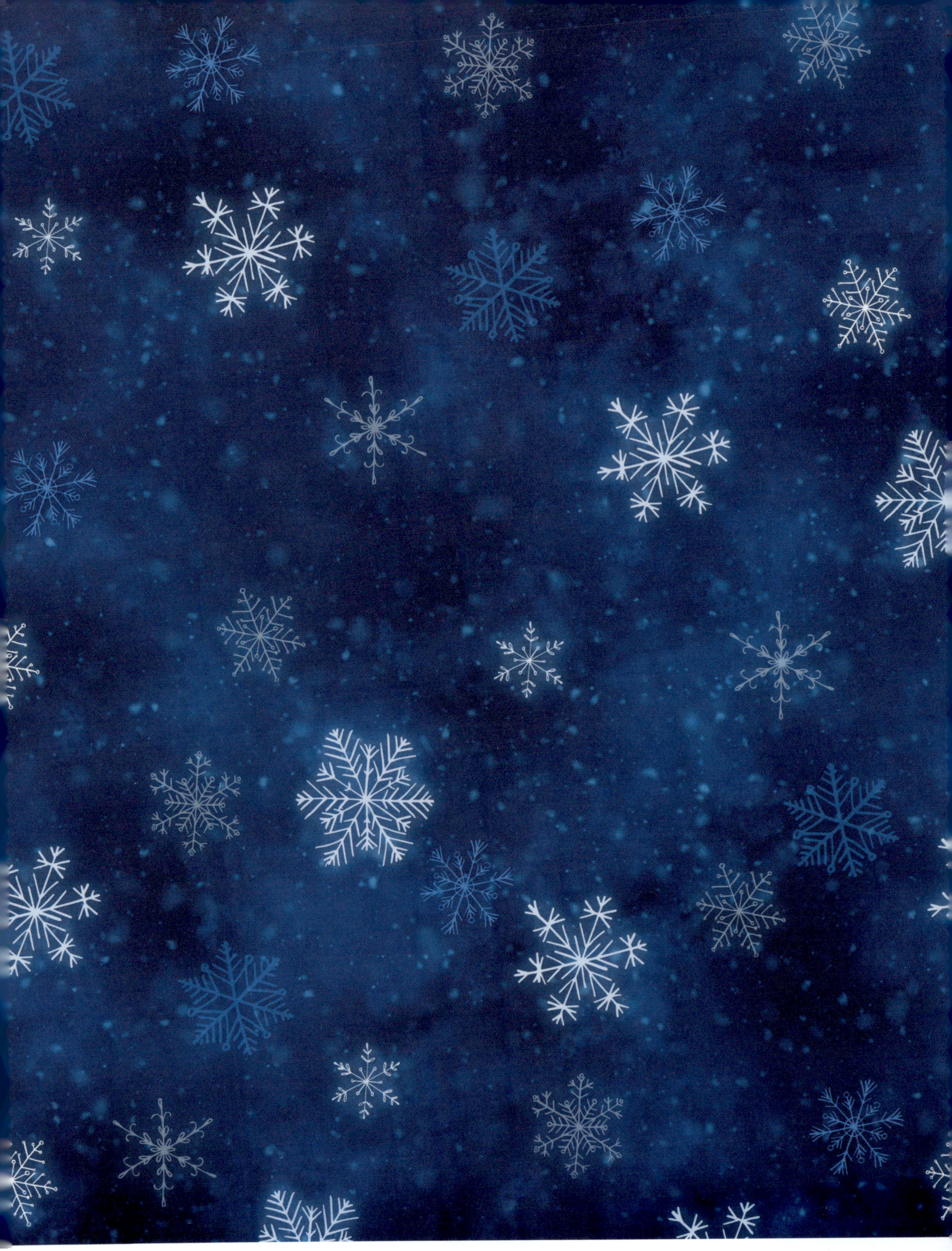

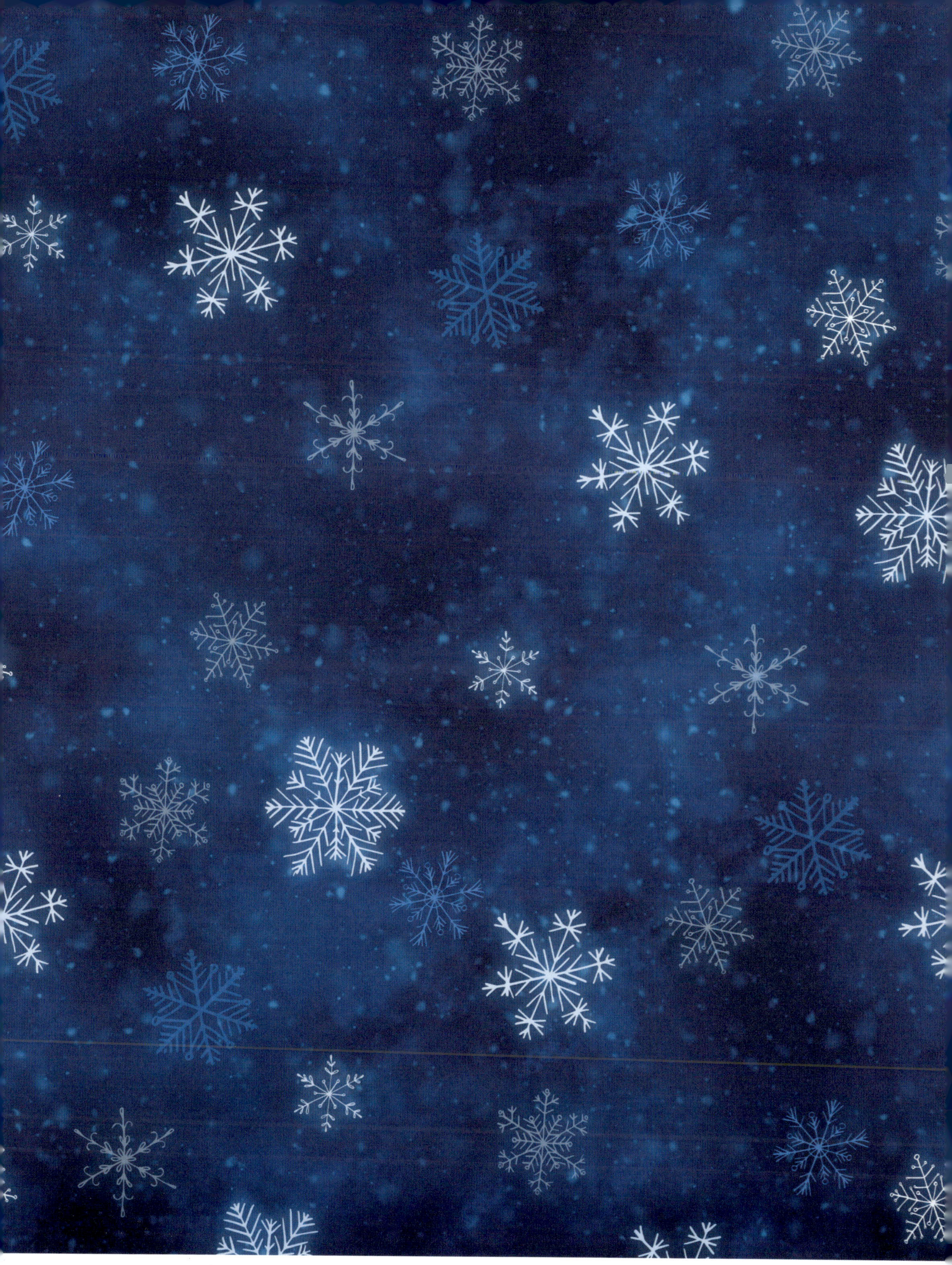

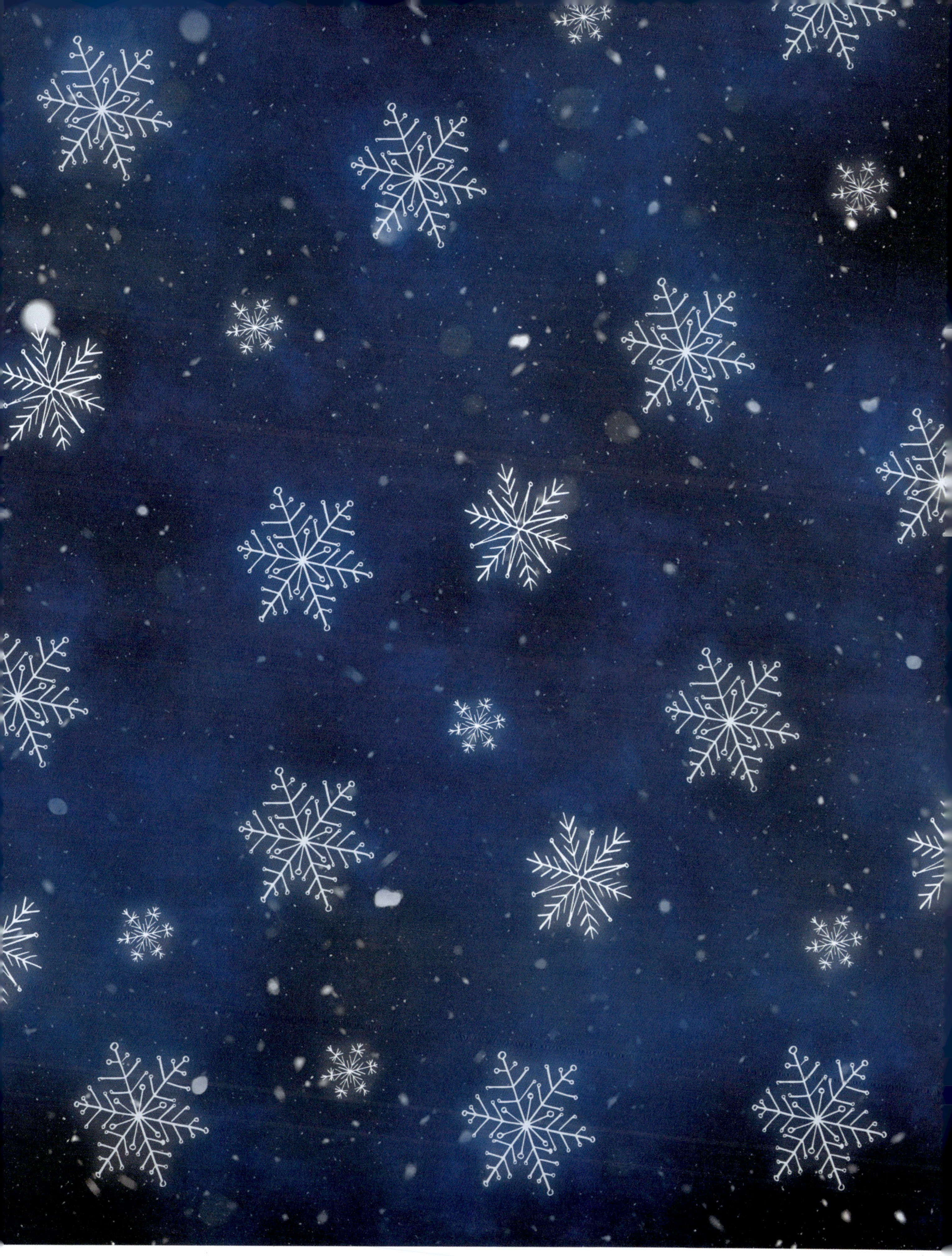

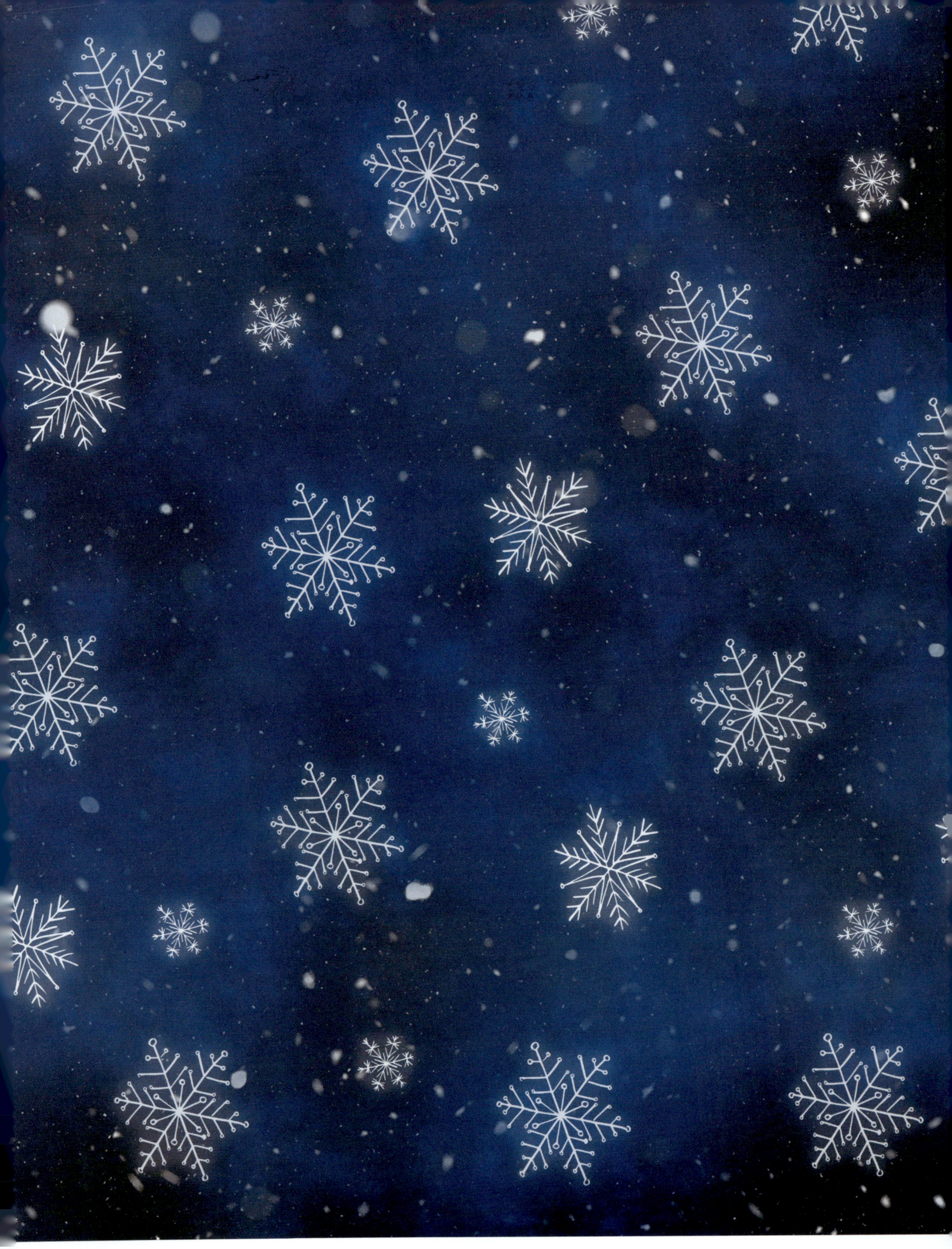

Printed in Great Britain
by Amazon

74975063R10024